Date Due

May 16	JUN 17 1995	
APR 12 1992	OCT 7 1997	
MAR 2 1 1986		
AUG 2 1984	JUL 17 1998	
AUG 14 1984		
APR 07 1986		
MAY 18 1986		
MAY 12 1989		
DEC 23 1994		
OCT 5 1998		

In the 1860s Great Britain's largest North American colony, the Province of Canada, had become ungovernable because of the conflicting aims of English- and French-Canadians. Worried about the need to defend the country from possible American aggression, interested in expansion westward across the continent and in consolidation of the railway system, Canadian politicians formed a coalition government to attempt to unite all the British North American colonies. In conferences at Charlottetown and Quebec in 1864, the Canadians and delegates from the Maritime provinces of Nova Scotia, New Brunswick, Prince Edward Island, and Newfoundland drew up the bases for a British North American union. The Maritime provinces at first rejected the scheme. New Brunswick and Nova Scotia finally agreed to join when heavy pressure from Britain was applied at the same time that American Fenians were threatening to invade the colonies. On July 1, 1867, the British North America Act created the Dominion of Canada, a new nation dominating half a continent.

PRINCIPALS

JOHN A. MACDONALD, the not always sober Upper Canadian Tory leader who became the master builder of Confederation and the Dominion's first prime minister.

GEORGE BROWN, outspoken leader of the Reformers who made Confederation possible by agreeing to join Macdonald in the Coalition of 1864.

GEORGE-ETIENNE CARTIER, *Chef* of the French-Canadians who guarded their interests at all times during the Confederation movement.

ALEXANDER TILLOCH GALT, a Lower Canadian businessman, the financial expert of the Coalition.

CHARLES TUPPER, the ambitious premier of Nova Scotia who played a waiting game until the time was ripe to rush Confederation through his legislature.

SAMUEL LEONARD TILLEY, premier of New Brunswick, "a deft trimmer" who was defeated on Confederation in 1865, but triumphantly re-elected in 1866.

JOSEPH HOWE, ex-premier of Nova Scotia and leader of the anti-Confederates, who considered Confederation the "Botheration Scheme."

A. J. SMITH, anti-Confederate premier of New Brunswick in 1865–1866 who found no alternative and was defeated.

THE FENIANS, wild American Irishmen, also fathers of Confederation.

CONFEDERATION

CONFEDERATION 1867
The Creation of the Dominion of Canada

By Michael Bliss

A World Focus Book

FRANKLIN WATTS, INC.
NEW YORK | 1975

For James, Laura, and Sara

Frontispiece: a Robert Harris painting showing the Fathers of Confederation at the Quebec Conference, 1864

Cover by Hernandez/Krenitsky
Maps by Vantage Art Inc.

Grateful acknowledgment is made to THE PUBLIC ARCHIVES OF CANADA for providing all the photographs and prints appearing in this volume.

Library of Congress Cataloging in Publication Data

Bliss, Michael.
    Confederation, 1867.

    (A World focus book)
    Bibliography: p.
    Includes index.
    SUMMARY: Describes the events leading to the Confederation of various Canadian provinces to become the Dominion of Canada.
    1. Canada—Politics and government—1841–1867—Juvenile literature. [1. Canada—History—1763–1867] I. Title.
F1032.B65   971.04   75–9721
ISBN 0–531–02173–4

Contents

BY THE QUEEN.

A PROCLAMATION

For Uniting the Provinces of Canada, Nova Scotia, and New Brunswick into One Dominion under the Name of CANADA.

VICTORIA R.

WHEREAS by an Act of Parliament passed on the Twenty-ninth Day of March One thousand eight hundred and sixty-seven, in the Thirtieth Year of Our Reign, intituled " An Act for the Union of Canada, Nova Scotia, and New Brunswick, and the " Government thereof, and for Purposes connected therewith," after divers Recitals, it is enacted, that " it shall be lawful for the Queen, by and with the Advice of Her Majesty's most Honorable " Privy Council, to declare by Proclamation that on and after a Day therein appointed, not being " more than Six Months after the passing of this Act, the Provinces of Canada, Nova Scotia, and " New Brunswick shall form and be One Dominion under the Name of Canada, and on and after " that Day those Three Provinces shall form and be One Dominion under that Name accordingly:" And it is thereby further enacted, that " such Persons shall be first summoned to the Senate as " the Queen, by Warrant under Her Majesty's Royal Sign Manual, thinks fit to approve, and " their Names shall be inserted in the Queen's Proclamation of Union:" We therefore, by and with the Advice of Our Privy Council, have thought fit to issue this Our Royal Proclamation, and We do Ordain, Declare, and Command, that on and after the First Day of July One thousand eight hundred and sixty-seven the Provinces of Canada, Nova Scotia, and New Brunswick shall form and be One Dominion under the Name of Canada. And We do further Ordain and Declare, that the Persons whose Names are herein inserted and set forth are the Persons of whom We have, by Warrant under Our Royal Sign Manual, thought fit to approve as the Persons who shall be first summoned to the Senate of Canada.

FOR THE PROVINCE OF ONTARIO.	FOR THE PROVINCE OF QUEBEC.	FOR THE PROVINCE OF NOVA SCOTIA.	FOR THE PROVINCE OF NEW BRUNSWICK.
JOHN HAMILTON,	JAMES LESLIE,	EDWARD KENNY,	AMOS EDWIN BOTSFORD,
RODERICK MATHESON,	ASA BELKNAP FOSTER,	JONATHAN M'CULLY,	EDWARD BARRON CHANDLER,
JOHN ROSS,	JOSEPH NOËL BOSSÉ,	THOMAS D. ARCHIBALD,	JOHN ROBERTSON,
SAMUEL MILLS,	LOUIS A. OLIVIER,	ROBERT B. DICKEY,	ROBERT LEONARD HAZEN,
BENJAMIN SEYMOUR,	JACQUE OLIVIER BUREAU,	JOHN H. ANDERSON,	WILLIAM HUNTER ODELL,
WALTER HAMILTON DICKSON,	CHARLES MALHIOT,	JOHN HOLMES,	DAVID WARK,
JAMES SHAW,	LOUIS RENAUD,	JOHN W. RITCHIE,	WILLIAM HENRY STEEVES,
ADAM JOHNSTON FERGUSON BLAIR,	LUC LETELLIER DE ST. JUST,	BENJAMIN WIER,	WILLIAM TODD,
ALEXANDER CAMPBELL,	ULRIC JOSEPH TESSIER,	JOHN LOCKE,	JOHN FERGUSON,
DAVID CHRISTIE,	JOHN HAMILTON,	CALEB R. BILL,	ROBERT DUNCAN WILMOT,
JAMES COX AIKINS,	CHARLES CORMIER,	JOHN BOURINOT,	ABNER REID M'CLELAN,
DAVID REESOR,	ANTOINE JUCHEREAU DUCHESNAY,	WILLIAM MILLER.	PETER MITCHELL.
ELIJAH LEONARD,	DAVID EDWARD PRICE,		
WILLIAM MACMASTER,	ELZEAR H. J. DUCHESNAY,		
ASA ALLWORTH BURNHAM,	LEANDRE DUMOUCHEL,		
JOHN SIMPSON,	LOUIS LACOSTE,		
JAMES SKEAD,	JOSEPH F. ARMAND,		
DAVID LEWIS MACPHERSON,	CHARLES WILSON,		
GEORGE CRAWFORD,	WILLIAM HENRY CHAFFERS,		
DONALD MACDONALD,	JEAN BAPTISTE GUÉVREMONT,		
OLIVER BLAKE,	JAMES FERRIER,		
BILLA FLINT,	Sir NARCISSE FORTUNAT BELLEAU, Knight,		
WALTER M'CREA,	THOMAS RYAN,		
GEORGE WILLIAM ALLAN.	JOHN SEWELL SANBORN.		

Given at Our Court at Windsor Castle, this Twenty-second Day of May, in the Year of our Lord One thousand eight hundred and sixty-seven, and in the Thirtieth Year of Our Reign.

God save the Queen.

LONDON: Printed by GEORGE EDWARD EYRE and WILLIAM SPOTTISWOODE, Printers to the Queen's most Excellent Majesty. 1867.

The Birth Day

The church bells rang at midnight. Guns roared from Halifax in the east to Sarnia in the west. Bonfires and fireworks lit the night in cities, towns, and villages a thousand miles apart. It was Monday, July 1, 1867, the first day in the history of the Dominion of Canada.

The bells pealed again at dawn; more salutes were fired. At church services special prayers were offered for the future of the new nation and its people. By 11:00 crowds had gathered in marketplaces and civic squares to hear the reading of the royal proclamation declaring that the British North America Act was in effect. Cheers went up for Canada and Queen Victoria; bands broke into "God Save the Queen." The military paraded in all their finery through streets lined with Union Jacks and banners offering "Success to the Confederacy," "Bienvenue A La Nouvelle Puissance."

The skies were clear and sunny across all four provinces. In Nova Scotia and New Brunswick a few disgruntled shopkeepers stayed open for business and black crepe was seen hanging from the windows of a few die-hard opponents of the Confederation. But most Canadians spent a happy afternoon "pic-nicking," playing cricket or lacrosse, watching the sailboat races in Halifax harbor, the harness races at the new course in Dunnville, the footraces at the park in Sherbrooke.

In Ottawa, John A. Macdonald took the oath of office to become Canada's first prime minister. A few minutes later he became Sir John A. Macdonald, knighted for his leadership in the Confederation movement. Back in Toronto, George Brown, the other statesman who had made the union possible, was sound asleep. He had been up all night writing the editorial for the Dominion Day edition of his newspaper, *The Globe*. "We

1

hail the birthday of a new nationality," it began. "A United British America, with its four millions of people, takes its place this day among the nations of the world." Some nine thousand words later Brown concluded with the ardent hope "that the people who now or shall hereafter inhabit the Dominion of Canada . . . who shall populate the northern part of the continent from the Atlantic to the Pacific, shall, under a wise and just government, reap the fruits of well directed enterprise, honest industry and religious principle . . . in the blessings of health, happiness, peace and prosperity. SO MOTE IT BE."

At dusk the horses and steamers and trains brought the holidayers home. But sleepy children were kept up past their bedtime to see the great bonfires flare again and the rockets and roman candles stream across the sky. The lights all finally died and the people drifted off to bed. Their country had been born.

A Few Acres of Snow

France and England were at war, the philosopher Voltaire wrote in 1759, "for a few acres of snow, and . . . they are spending for this fine war more than all Canada is worth." There were some Englishmen who shared his feelings. Even after the capital of New France, Quebec, had fallen to General Wolfe on the Plains of Abraham that year, the British seriously considered giving the country back to France in return for a sugar-producing island in the West Indies. They fortunately thought better of the trade, and by the Treaty of Paris of 1763 gained all the former French territories in North America, except for two small islands retained by France and the Louisiana Territory, which was given to Spain.

The first plan for dealing with the northern domain was to treat it just like the thirteen British colonies to the south. The British hoped that the restless citizens of these colonies would emigrate to the new provinces of Quebec and Nova Scotia, swamping the 65,000 French-speaking *Canadiens* who remained from France's fur-trading empire in North America.

Several thousand New Englanders did come to Nova Scotia, from which the French-speaking Acadians had been expelled in 1756. But Quebec remained so predominantly French in character that the British government recognized this in the Quebec Act of 1774 by granting religious equality to Roman Catholics and establishing the French code of civil laws in the province. There were already signs that the birthrate among the French-Canadians, one of the highest in the world, would guarantee them *la revanche du berceau,* the revenge of the cradle.

During the American Revolution (one of the contributing causes of which had been American hostility to the Quebec

3

Act), the ex-Yankees in Nova Scotia stayed neutral. A clumsy American invasion of Quebec was eventually repulsed by the British, as the French-Canadians showed little interest in the great issues dividing England and the thirteen colonies. After the war Nova Scotia and Quebec were the natural places of refuge for those Americans who remained loyal to King George III. In the mid-1780s some forty to fifty thousand United Empire Loyalists emigrated to the British North American provinces.

The main areas of Loyalist settlement were New Brunswick, carved out as a separate province from Nova Scotia in 1784 (St. John Island, later renamed Prince Edward Island, had also been made a separate province in 1769), and Upper Canada, created in 1791 when Quebec was divided into Upper and Lower Canada. Earlier, though, Quebec had lost the upper Mississippi valley when it was transferred to the United States by the 1783 Peace of Paris. The boundary between American and British territory now ran from the Bay of Fundy on the Atlantic, south of the St. Lawrence River system, through the midline of the Great Lakes, and west across the continent from the tip of Lake Superior.

The determination of the Loyalists to live as British subjects separate from the United States was tested during the War of 1812 between the United States and Britain. The successful defense of British North America from invasion strengthened the anti-American sentiments dominant in the colonies since the Revolution. At the same time it left their residents perpetually afraid that the Americans might try again another day.

The fur trade had been the basis of the economy of New France and continued as a staple industry of British North America until the 1820s. By then the great pine forests of New Brunswick and the Canadas were providing a new source of wealth to the colonists in the form of square timber exported to

The taking of Quebec,
September 13, 1759

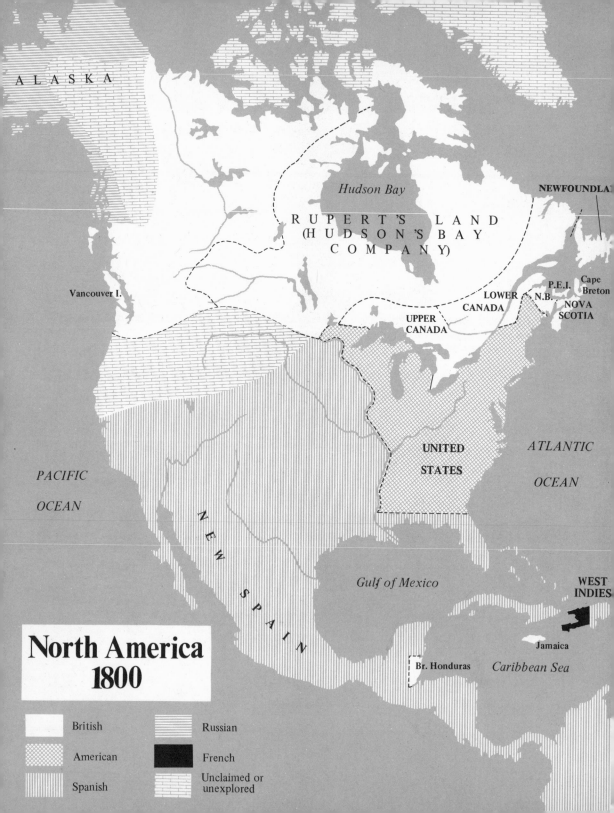

ALASKA

Hudson Bay

NEWFOUNDLA[ND]

R U P E R T ' S L A N D
(H U D S O N ' S B A Y
C O M P A N Y)

Vancouver I.

LOWER
CANADA

P.E.I.

Cape
Breton

N.B.

NOVA
SCOTIA

UPPER
CANADA

UNITED
STATES

ATLANTIC

OCEAN

PACIFIC

OCEAN

N
E
W

S
P
A
I
N

Gulf of Mexico

WEST
INDIES

Jamaica

Br. Honduras

Caribbean Sea

North America
1800

British	Russian
American	French
Spanish	Unclaimed or unexplored

England. As the land between the pre-Cambrian Shield and the Great Lakes was cleared, it proved well suited to agriculture. Upper Canada was soon exporting large quantities of grain and was the frontier to which most immigrants came. Some moved west from the United States, others emigrated from Britain; thousands of destitute, starving Irish poured in during the 1840s.

New Brunswick and Nova Scotia gradually developed extensive shipbuilding industries and thriving ports at Saint John and Halifax. The Nova Scotians became especially active in North Atlantic commerce, a truly Maritime community of "Bluenoses." Both Prince Edward Island, largely agricultural, and the old fishing settlement of Newfoundland were almost self-contained economically and tended to stay isolated from the rest of British North America.

In the 1820s and 1830s popular discontent developed in most of the colonies against the lack of true self-government. British governors and their advisers were not responsible to the local legislatures for their actions. Elected colonial politicians felt that the people's interests were being disregarded by small cliques of appointees from England. Feelings were particularly bitter in Lower Canada where the French-Canadian majority was becoming deeply conscious of its separate identity and determined to preserve it against the aggressive British merchant community of Montreal.

The British government was willing to respond to colonial grievances, but did not move quickly enough to prevent the outbreak of rebellions in Upper and Lower Canada in 1837. It was largely a comic-opera affair in Upper Canada, but much more serious in the lower province, where political discontent symbolized deep racial division.

As a result of the rebellions, Upper and Lower Canada were united into one colony, the Province of Canada, in 1841.

*American invaders checked
at Stoney Creek during
the War of 1812*

The two sections of the province were each given equal representation in the legislative assembly to guarantee that the French of Lower Canada would not hold majority power. More important, in the late 1840s Britain gradually conceded the right of responsible government to all its North American colonies. Governors were to choose as ministers only those politicians who had the confidence of a majority in the assembly. The threat of resignation by the ministers, and thus an impasse between the governor and the assembly, would be sufficient to ensure that their advice was taken. Responsible government meant colonial self-government in all but a few areas of particular concern to the mother country, such as defense and external affairs. It was the colonies' first big step toward their eventual independence.

By the middle decades of the nineteenth century, Voltaire's "few acres of snow" had become settled, prosperous, self-governing communities. Their economy based on "wood, wind, and water," Nova Scotians and New Brunswickers were among the leading seafaring people of the world. The Canadians thought they were the greatest railroaders in the world, for, in addition to a splendid canal system along the St. Lawrence River, by 1858 their province also had the world's longest railway, the 1,100-mile-long Grand Trunk, forming a backbone to the province from Quebec City to Sarnia. Iron foundries, farm-implement factories, and textile mills were beginning to produce goods "made in Canada." A reciprocity treaty with the United States in 1854 ensured a ready market for surplus lumber, fish, and agricultural products produced in all the colonies, easing anxiety about the loss of a favored position in British markets when the mother country had decided to trade freely with everyone in the 1840s.

By 1861 there were more than 3 million British North

HUDSON

BAY

Rupert's

(HUDSON'S BAY

L. SUPERIOR

UPPER

Province of

CANADA

LOWER

L.
MICHIGAN

• Sudbury

Ottawa R.

Georgian
Bay

L. HURON

St. Lawrence

Montreal

Richmond

Ottawa •

Sherbrooke

Grand Trunk Ry.

Kingston

Toronto

Guelph •

L. ONTARIO

Sarnia •

London •

• Hamilton

• Windsor

• Buffalo

L. ERIE

UNITED STATES

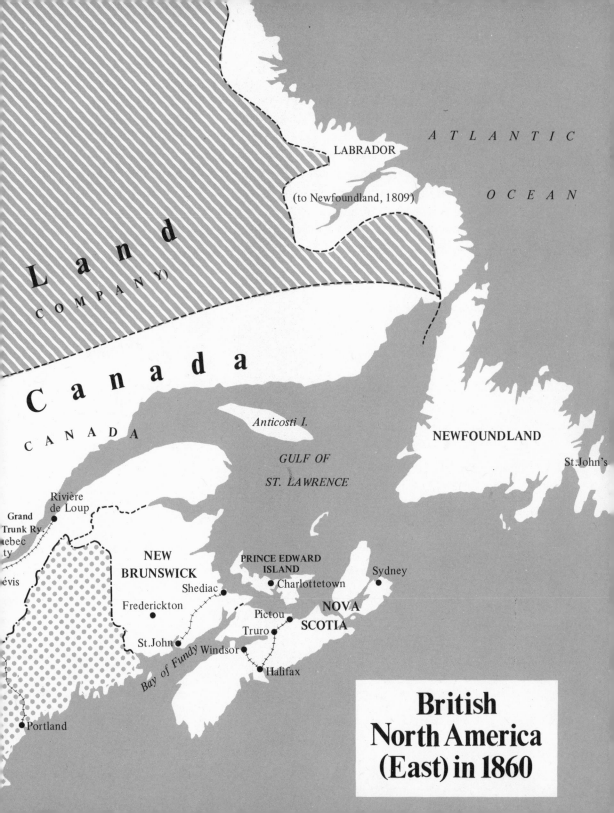

ATLANTIC

OCEAN

LABRADOR

(to Newfoundland, 1809)

L a n d

COMPANY)

C a n a d a

CANADA

Anticosti I.

*GULF OF
ST. LAWRENCE*

NEWFOUNDLAND

St.John's

Rivière
de Loup

Grand
Trunk Ry.
ebec
ty

évis

**NEW
BRUNSWICK**

**PRINCE EDWARD
ISLAND**

Shediac

Charlottetown

Sydney

Frederickton

Pictou

**NOVA
SCOTIA**

St.John

Truro

Bay of Fundy Windsor

Halifax

Portland

**British
North America
(East) in 1860**

Americans living in Canada and the Maritime provinces of Nova Scotia, New Brunswick, Prince Edward Island, and Newfoundland; and a handful more in the wild lands north and west of the Great Lakes governed by the Hudson's Bay Company. Communications were still primitive. Few Canadians knew anything about Maritimers and vice versa. There was no sense of a common identity. But already a few British North Americans were beginning to dream about a day when the separate colonies might be united into one great nation.

Troubled Colonies

In the late 1850s and early 1860s a set of circumstances developed that made the idea of uniting British North America into something more than a dream. Consolidation gradually began to appear to offer significant political, military, and economic advantages. As more and more politicians understood this, what at first seemed like an idealistic vision became a practical possibility.

For one thing, the Province of Canada wasn't working very well. There had never been much love lost between the Protestant Anglo-Saxons of Upper Canada and the Roman Catholic French-Canadians of Lower Canada. As immigration swelled the population of Upper Canada, the equal representation in the assembly given the two sections in 1841 (designed then to limit the power of the French) now seemed a device that allowed the French of Lower Canada to have more representatives in the government than their numbers warranted. Shouldn't the larger section of the province have the most members of the assembly? Representation by population, or "Rep by Pop," became the rallying slogan of the Reform party that dominated Upper Canada, led by the fiery Scots editor of *The Globe,* George Brown. It was the only way, he thought, that Canada could free itself from "Papal domination" of its politics by the French-Canadians in alliance with a few Upper Canadian Tories.

In Lower Canada the French-Canadians were naturally fearful that any loss of representation would pave the way for an attack on their religious and legal institutions, perhaps on their very language itself. The conservative *Bleu* party of Lower Canada, led by George-Etienne Cartier, firmly resisted any change in the constitution. His chief English-speaking ally was John A. Macdonald, leader of the Tory minority from Upper

Canada. Macdonald was an easygoing if often hard-drinking politician, who tended to believe that if the status quo were preserved long enough, something would turn up.

By the early 1860s something had to turn up, for the province was locked in political stalemate. In the assembly the Reform majority of Upper Canada plus the *Rouges* minority from Lower Canada almost exactly equaled the combination of the Upper Canadian Tories and Lower Canadian *Bleus*. In that situation no government could long retain control of a majority of votes. By the spring of 1864 the province had had two elections and three changes of government in three years and there was still no prospect of breaking the deadlock—unless, many were starting to say, Upper and Lower Canada were separated again into two provinces, so English and French could go their separate ways.

But many Canadians were also beginning to call for expansion of the province, not its dissolution. The province badly needed new frontiers of settlement, for most of the fertile land in the Upper Canadian peninsula had been cleared. To the north the Canadian Shield was vast, and perhaps even rich in natural resources, but quite unsuited to farming. Where could farmers' sons go to find virgin land of their own? Would it have to be to the United States, where many were starting to move in the 1850s? What about the millions of acres of flat, treeless prairie north and west of the Great Lakes, the Northwest Territories Britain had let the Hudson's Bay Company govern? If these could be annexed to Canada, it would have a new frontier,

Above: George Brown
Below: John A. Macdonald

indeed an almost boundless new empire stretching to the foot-hills of the Rocky Mountains.

The idea of a Canadian "manifest destiny" to expand west-ward did not appeal strongly to French-Canadians, though. They correctly believed that they would have little share in emigration to the Northwest, and worried that it was another scheme by which the Upper Canadian Protestants (especially George Brown and his Reformers, who were most interested in the Northwest) would increase their power. The *Bleu*-Tory party would have nothing to do with it. So unless the stalemate in Canadian politics could be broken, there was little likelihood of western expansion becoming a practical possibility.

Another reason why the province had to be kept strong, and possibly made even stronger, was the debt it had incurred building its fine railway system. The Grand Trunk had been generously aided by the provincial government but still found it could not pay its way, and by 1860 it was teetering on the brink of bankruptcy. Many railroaders, including the Grand Trunk's own management, thought the solution to its problems would be to build still more railways, perhaps a railway right across the continent if the Northwest could be acquired, certainly an Inter-colonial Railway to link Canada with Nova Scotia and New Brunswick.

Many *Bleu* and Tory politicians were sympathetic to the plight of the Grand Trunk. Reformers were not. Here was an-other Canadian problem snarled in the web of political deadlock.

The idea of an Intercolonial Railway also interested the British North Americans in the Atlantic provinces. In the 1850s some three hundred miles of local railway had been built in New Brunswick and Nova Scotia. The whole cost had been paid by the provincial governments and the burden of debt was mount-ing annually. As in the Province of Canada, the only salvation for the local systems seemed to be to link them with a railway connecting the seaports of Halifax and Saint John with the interior of the continent. For almost twenty years the colonies had been trying to agree with the imperial government on the details for financing an Intercolonial. What seemed to be a final arrangement fell apart in 1863, causing considerable bad feeling between Maritimers and "perfidious" Canadians. But it was still true that Maritimers would listen eagerly to any plan that would give their seacoast provinces the long-desired link with the heartland of Canada.

One plan some of them were considering in the early 1860s was the idea of uniting Nova Scotia, New Brunswick, and Prince Edward Island into one province with a government strong enough to carry on its own railway projects. Maritime Union, as the proposal was called, would also ease the pettiness, corruption, and expense involved in keeping three small colonial governments going when one could do just as well. Under considerable pressure from their British governors, the legislatures of Nova Scotia, New Brunswick, and Prince Edward Island agreed in the spring of 1864 to call a conference to consider Maritime Union.

British North Americans were considering all these problems with an added sense of urgency because of the terrible American Civil War that had been raging to their south since 1861. One of that war's earliest side effects had been to strain relations between the United States and Great Britain because of supposed British sympathies with the Confederate states. There was a serious danger of war in 1862 in the aftermath of the *Trent* affair when Americans seized two Confederate agents traveling on a British warship. Fifteen thousand British troops were rushed to North America to help strengthen the colonies' defenses in the event of war. Because the St. Lawrence was

British troops passing through
New Brunswick to strengthen
British North American
defenses against a feared
American invasion, 1862

frozen, they had to march overland from New Brunswick to Quebec in bitter winter cold. It was additional proof of the need for an Intercolonial Railway.

Other incidents along the border and on the high seas kept tensions high. Nor had British North Americans forgotten the invasions of 1812–1814 or the Oregon crisis of 1844 when they seemed about to become the victims of aggressive American expansion. They worried about American designs on the Northwest—already Minnesota was calling for its annexation—and wondered whether it would be possible to defend their territory after the war if the battle-hardened Union armies were sent north.

The causes of the Confederation of 1867 are sometimes difficult to understand because so many factors seemed to be at work: political deadlock in the Province of Canada, desires for western expansion, the problems of the Grand Trunk and the need for an Intercolonial, fears of the United States. None of these was *the* most significant cause of Confederation. Instead, the various problems were like logs that had gradually jammed up in the stream of British North American history. Some one event was needed to break the jam and resolve all the outstanding issues—political, economic, and military.

Going Down to Charlottetown

The deadlock was broken in the Province of Canada on June 22, 1864. John A. Macdonald and George Cartier announced that their deadly political enemies, George Brown and his Reformers, were joining them in a Coalition ministry. The new government's first item of business would be to try to interest the Maritime colonies in a British North American federation. The Coalition had heard that a conference was to be called to discuss Maritime Union. Could Canada send delegates to discuss the larger question?

George Brown should be given much of the credit for the formation of the Coalition. By 1864 he had realized that "Rep by Pop" simply would not be accepted by the French-Canadians. They had to have some assurance of protection for their language and culture in any new constitution. An ardent advocate of western expansion, he also knew that his political opponents would not accept acquiring the Hudson's Bay Company's territories unless the railway situation was also solved at the same time. He was tired of politics (he was now happily married and anxious to spend time with his family; Anne Brown has been called "the Mother of Confederation"), and offered to join a coalition in the hope that all politicians could work together to solve the outstanding problems of British North America. Then he could retire to his newspaper and his happy home life.

John A. Macdonald had also realized that the status quo in the Province of Canada had no future. Until the last moment he had been cool to the idea of a larger British North American union. As ever, though, he was shrewd enough to jump on a passing bandwagon. And he was the kind of politician who had a knack of always ending up as the leader of the band.

The Maritimers had not yet chosen dates or a place for their conference on Maritime Union. It might not even have been held if the Canadians had not invited themselves along. When the request came from Canada, though, hasty preparations were made to hold a conference at Charlottetown, the capital of Prince Edward Island, in September. The Canadians would be welcome unofficial visitors.

A powerful and well-prepared Canadian delegation of eight ministers left Quebec City on the steamer *Queen Victoria* on August 29. Brown and Macdonald had been the dominant figures in Canadian politics for the past ten years. Cartier was acknowledged as the unrivaled *chef* of the French-Canadians. Alexander Tilloch Galt, an experienced businessman and the Coalition's financial expert, had been urging a union since 1858. The most outstanding of the junior ministers was Thomas D'Arcy McGee, an Irish ex-rebel who became known as the "poet of Confederation" for his writing and speeches.

The *Queen Victoria* dropped anchor in Charlottetown harbor at noon on September 1. Its passengers were a little surprised that the reception committee consisted only of one Island official in an oyster boat. Most of Charlottetown's seven thousand citizens were more interested in the clowns and trick horses featured by Slaymaker & Nichols Olympic Circus, the first to visit their island in twenty years.

The conference opened that afternoon in the Legislative Council chamber of the Colonial Building. The fifteen delegates from Prince Edward Island, Nova Scotia, and New Brunswick soon decided to hear what their guests had to say before seriously considering Maritime Union. The Canadians were invited in, and after "the shake elbow & the How d'ye do & the fine weather" it was agreed the conference would listen to their proposal.

Reporters were not present at the Charlottetown Conference and it was not until 1967 that a few scrawled minutes of some of the sessions were discovered. Historians have only vague and conflicting accounts of who spoke on which day and what subjects were discussed. We do know that the Canadians were the center of attention from Friday, September 2, through Tuesday the sixth.

They seemed wonderfully sure of themselves—Macdonald, Cartier, Galt, and Brown—as they outlined their detailed plan for a new political structure for all of British North America, the formation of a new nation. It would be a federation. There would be a powerful central government, but the provinces, like American states, would retain their identity and their own local legislatures. Maritimers could first unite into one big province if they wished, or possibly they could enter the Confederation as separate provinces. Great projects like railway construction and western expansion could be carried out by the central government, but local interests would be protected both in the new parliamentary structure and by the continuance of the provincial legislatures.

In any case the details could be argued out later. All the Maritimers needed to do was agree that the scheme could work, that the time to form the new nation was now, not in the vague and distant future. Once that was accepted, another conference could be held to do the hard work of drawing up a draft constitution.

There were dinners and entertainment for the guests every evening. Perhaps the real climax of the Charlottetown Conference came on Saturday afternoon when all the delegates had a "princely" luncheon on board the *Queen Victoria,* which had been well stocked with champagne before it left Quebec. George Brown described the occasion to his wife:

Cartier & I made eloquent speeches—of course—& whether as the result of our eloquence or of the goodness of our champagne, the ice became completely broken, the tongues of the delegates wagged merrily, and the banns of matrimony between all the Provinces of BNA having been formally proclaimed & all manner of persons duly warned then & there to speak or forever after to hold their tongues —no man appeared to forbid the banns & the union was thereupon formally completed & proclaimed.

More soberly, the delegates from Nova Scotia, New Brunswick, and Prince Edward Island decided on Wednesday the sixth to postpone their discussion of Maritime Union. Most of them were convinced that a wider union would be desirable if it were practical. At least there was nothing to lose in meeting again with the Canadians. With that the Charlottetown Conference adjourned. All the delegates, including the Canadians, went off to Halifax and then to Saint John and Fredericton in New Brunswick for dinners, speech-making, and discussions of whether Maritime Union should come before or after a Confederation.

Over: the delegates at the Charlottetown Conference, September, 1864. John A. Macdonald is sitting on the step in the center; Cartier is standing on his right.

At midnight on September 16 the Canadians boarded the *Queen Victoria* to go home. The Maritimers had accepted their invitation to come to Quebec in October to hold an official conference on Confederation. This was exactly what they had wanted. "We have got on very amicably—we Canadians—wonderfully so!" Brown wrote to Anne. "Our expedition has been all and more than we could have hoped."

George Brown might have been a bit less optimistic had he heard Prince Edward Islanders talking to one another when their delegates passed by during the conference. "There go the men," it was said, "who would sell their country."

Constitution-making
at Quebec

On October 10, 1864, thirty-three British North American politicians sat down in Quebec City to draft a constitution for a new nation. They met in an undistinguished government building in the upper city, high on the cliffs overlooking the St. Lawrence, only a few hundred yards from the Plains of Abraham. The Maritime delegates had brought their wives and daughters, and everyone hoped for a repetition of the fine weather and convivial atmosphere of Charlottetown.

It was rainy, muddy, and cold throughout the Quebec Conference. And although there was no shortage of wine and spirits, or of balls and dinner parties, the men spent long evenings haggling over the complexities of representation and the division of powers. After two and a half weeks' work they produced seventy-two resolutions outlining a political structure for a new British North American nation. But when they were finished they could no longer be so certain that everyone would accept "the banns of matrimony between all the Provinces."

On many vital issues there was complete agreement among the delegates at Quebec. Their provinces made up *British* North America, and none of them doubted that it would remain British. Confederation, if it could be achieved, would be a coming together of British provinces or colonies into one large British province or colony (or nation, or some other term). It would not be—and was not—a step toward independence from Britain. Perhaps a few of the delegates did dream of a day when a new North American nation would be an equal partner with Britain in the Empire, but hardly anyone in the 1860s was interested in independence.

Nor would it be necessary for Canada's "founding fathers" to devise a new system of government the way the Americans had. Everyone agreed that "the well understood principles of the British constitution" would be the model that should be followed "as far as our circumstances will permit." There would be no complicated system of checks and balances comparable to the American Constitution—indeed, not very many of the democratic characteristics of the American republic. Or, rather, the *two* American republics, because nothing was so obvious about the American system in those Civil War years than its failure to keep Americans united as one happy people. The example of the United States influenced the Fathers of Confederation chiefly as a model of what to avoid.

But they could not avoid following American practice in one important way. The union would have to be a *federal* union, that is, one with two levels of government. The central or national government would be given authority over all matters of national interest, everything to do with the provision of "peace, welfare, and good government." But the provinces would survive, each with its own legislature, to deal with matters of local interest.

Most of the English-speaking delegates to the Quebec Conference would have preferred a *legislative* union, like that of the United Kingdom, in which there was only one government for the whole nation. But everyone realized that the French-Canadians would never agree to surrender control of their cultural institutions. They had to have a provincial legislature, in which they would be predominant, to protect their language, religion, and legal code. Similarly, there were many in the Maritimes who were reluctant to see their provincial assemblies disappear and to have all their affairs directed by a government a thousand miles away (no one ever doubted that Ottawa, capital of the Province of Canada, would be the capital of the new nation) run by Upper and Lower Canadians. In general, the union would encompass too much territory, too many different regions, and too many groups of people with conflicting interests for one level of government to handle effectively.

Most of the disagreements at Quebec revolved around how the federal system should work. The central Parliament would have two "houses," as in Britain and the United States. Representatives to the lower house, the House of Commons, would be elected on the basis of population—"Rep by Pop," George Brown's great principle. The members of the upper house were to be appointed for life. Like the House of Lords in England they would act as a sobering influence on the democratically chosen House of Commons. But the upper house was also expected to function like the American Senate as a safeguard for local or sectional interests in the central government. In fact, it was finally named the Senate. Its members would be appointed on some kind of sectional basis. But what kind?

In the new union the old Province of Canada would be divided into two provinces. The Maritimes would come in either as separate provinces, or, if Maritime Union came about, as one province. The American model of giving each state equal representation in the Senate was not followed. Each "section"—Upper Canada, Lower Canada, and the Maritimes—would have equal representation in the upper house.

Many Maritimers felt this was unjust because it meant that their three provinces—perhaps even four, because Newfoundland had sent delegates to Quebec—would be outvoted by a 2 to 1 majority in the Senate by the representatives from the two sections of Canada. The Quebec Conference spent three days arguing about the details of representation in the upper house before a compromise was worked out that did not change the basic principle.

Another contentious issue was the division of powers between the central government and the provinces. John A. Macdonald, who emerged at Quebec as the master builder of the Canadian Constitution, was determined to give as little power to the provinces as possible. Like many British North Americans, he felt the American Constitution had given too much power to the states and that the doctrine of "States' Rights" had been a major cause of the Civil War. So in his proposals the central government would have all powers not specifically given to the provinces (in the American Constitution these "residual powers" went to the states), and the central government would also be able to disallow *any* legislation passed by a provincial government. These, plus several other provisions strengthening the central government, meant that the new union would be a highly centralized federation, one in which the provincial role would be reduced to a minimum.

These proposals were eventually accepted, but not without long objections from those Maritimers, especially the Prince Edward Island delegates, who felt they were being asked to surrender their right of self-government and that their local interests would be lost sight of in the new union.

Finally, there had to be hard bargaining over the financial rearrangements accompanying the union. Galt had worked out an ingenious scheme for the central government to take over all the debts of the old provinces along with most of their sources of revenue. At the same time it would provide subsidies based on population to the new provincial governments to help pay their expenses. This was generally acceptable, but there were subtle details to be ironed out. Each delegation was anxious to get the best possible financial terms for its province. Again, the Prince Edward Islanders felt that the final terms were not very satisfactory because they did not take into account the Island's special needs.

George Cartier and the other French-Canadians were not very active in the Quebec discussions, possibly because they felt everyone was already taking account of the special French fact in Canada. Certainly there was no debate on the resolution providing that both English and French would be official languages in the central Parliament, the federal courts, and the courts and legislature of Lower Canada. Canadian historians still cannot agree, however, on whether the Fathers of Confederation were giving only limited recognition to the French language or whether they foresaw a fully bilingual and bicultural nation emerging out of the union.

There is no doubt that the Fathers of Confederation did foresee the union expanding into a transcontinental nation. Provision was made in the Quebec Resolutions for the admission of new provinces and territories, particularly the Northwest, and for the improvement of communications with the west. The Intercolonial Railway was also to be built "without delay." If union was achieved, then, the new government would immediately carry out the two developments that most interested British North Americans—western expansion and a railway link between the Maritimes and the central provinces.

If! There was no guarantee that the Quebec Resolutions would be the constitution of a new union. Britain was known to favor the project but would not pass the required legislation unless all the provinces gave their consent. The delegates to Quebec did not officially speak for their provinces. It was really only

a conference of interested politicians, without any official standing. Having drawn up their resolutions, the delegates would have to take them back to their provincial legislatures for approval. Perhaps it was still a little early to think of them as Fathers of Confederation. The scheme had been conceived, but it could also be aborted.

Above: George-Etienne Cartier
Below: Alexander Tilloch Galt

Setbacks

The initiative for Confederation had come from the Province of Canada. It was the main plank in the Coalition government's platform and, as such, had the support of an overwhelming majority in the legislature. There was never any serious question of the legislature's approval.

Some critics of the plan suggested that it should be submitted to the people in a special election or at least a plebiscite. Had this been done, it is at least possible that a majority of French-Canadians would have opposed Confederation. Many of them felt that the existing balance of power in the Province best preserved their rights, and that the strong central government envisaged in the Quebec Resolutions would be a menace to their survival.

The government did not feel that the people should vote directly on Confederation. In a British system, the people's representatives in the legislature made decisions and accepted responsibility for them. Taking Confederation to the people would be unnecessary, unduly democratic, and perhaps even fatal to the project. As for the French-Canadians, Cartier and his *Bleu* supporters in the legislature favored the scheme. There was no reason to go beyond them and test public opinion.

In February and March, 1865, the Canadian legislature held a month-long debate on the Quebec Resolutions. It was a wide-ranging, brilliant discussion, with the best speeches coming from the government leaders, Macdonald, Brown, Cartier, and McGee. There were also perceptive criticisms, especially from the *Rouges* of Lower Canada who supplied most of the opposition. One of the most telling points made inside and outside the legislature referred to the proposed division of authority. To those who favored a legislative union the leaders of Confederation stressed the weakness of the proposed provincial governments; it was really a legislative union in disguise, they seemed to be saying. But when other critics, particularly French-Canadians, objected to this feature, they were assured that the provinces had very large powers, everything that was needed to handle all their local interests. Skilled politicians as they were, the leaders of Confederation in Canada were adept at talking out of both sides of their mouths when it suited them.

Whatever the uncertainties about how the system might work in the future, the Quebec Resolutions and the Confederation scheme offered so many advantages to the Province of Canada—"Rep by Pop," western expansion, railway development—that the outcome of the debate was never in doubt. At 4:30 A.M. on Saturday, March 11, 1865, the legislative assembly of Canada approved the Quebec Resolutions by a vote of 91–33.

But the members' cheers when the vote was announced may have been a little fainthearted. For by then it was clear that whatever Canada might do about Confederation, the movement was in serious trouble in the Maritimes.

The Prince Edward Islanders had been obviously unhappy at Quebec, defeated time and time again on suggestions that would give their little island more influence in the new union. When the delegates went home to Charlottetown in the fall of 1864, they fell to bickering among themselves as to whether the Quebec Resolutions were a reasonable basis for union. They also found that public opinion was strongly against change of any kind. What did the Islanders, many of whom had never visited the mainland, care about new western territories thousands of miles away? Why should they pay more taxes to build an Intercolonial Railway that obviously wouldn't run on the Island? They were self-governing; Charlottetown, their capital, was no more than a day's buggy ride from any point on the Island. Why turn their affairs over to a government somewhere in the wilds of Canada, inevitably dominated by Upper and Lower Canadians?

The premier of the Island, who supported Confederation, was forced to resign in December, giving way to an anti-Confederate ministry. Everyone knew that Prince Edward Island, where Confederation had been born, was out of the scheme, at least for the time being.

Nor was there much hope from the other island, Newfoundland. Its two observers at Quebec had seemed to favor Confederation, but when they went home they were met with a combination of apathy and ignorance. Newfoundland was a poverty-stricken fishing station in the Atlantic. Confederation seemed to offer nothing to its people (except, one critic claimed, the prospect of "leaving their bones to bleach on a foreign land" defending Canada from the United States), and they had nothing to offer to Confederation. Fearing defeat, the Newfoundland government did not bring Confederation to a vote in the legislature.

These defections from the cause were disturbing but not critical. Neither Newfoundland nor Prince Edward Island was vital to the plan. They could go off on their own and perhaps be brought in later. What was absolutely essential was the agreement of both New Brunswick and Nova Scotia. But as the winter of 1864–1865 deepened, this seemed increasingly unlikely.

The two premiers, Dr. Charles Tupper of Nova Scotia and Samuel Leonard Tilley of New Brunswick, had become com-

Above: Charles Tupper
Below: Samuel Leonard Tilley

mitted to Confederation at Charlottetown and Quebec. Tupper, an ambitious, gambling man, and Tilley, "a deft trimmer, clever and adroit," were both restless for greater scope for their talents. They seized the opportunity to participate in the making of what might one day be a great and powerful nation. Most of the other delegates from their provinces, including prominent opposition politicians, also came back from the conferences as converts to Confederation.

But political parties were still in their infancy in the 1860s, and leaders could not count on the support of their supposed followers, particularly when other prominent politicians came out against Confederation.

To Joseph Howe, ex-premier of Nova Scotia and the best-known public figure in the Maritimes, Confederation was the "Botheration Scheme." He came out in opposition to it early in 1865, joining a mounting wave of critical comment in both provinces. Some have said Howe was acting only out of jealousy of Tupper. In fact, like many Maritime politicians and businessmen, Howe was genuinely concerned that Confederation would be disastrous to the region.

The Maritime provinces raised most of their revenue from tariffs or customs duties. If they were united with the other provinces, the central government would control the tariff. Maritime anti-Confederates thought a new tariff would be much higher than their old one, and their provinces would have to bear a crushing burden of taxation. For surely the Canadians would dominate the new union, and what real concern did they have for Nova Scotia and New Brunswick?

Joseph Howe on the platform
addressing a meeting

What did Maritimers and Canadians have in common any-way? Culturally and economically Nova Scotia at least was closer to London, the heart of the world's greatest empire, than it was to Ottawa, the backwoods capital of Canada. The Maritime communities were reasonably prosperous and satisfied with their self-government. The Province of Canada was racially divided, deeply in debt, apparently ungovernable. "A more unpromising nucleus of a new nation can hardly be found on the face of the earth," Howe thundered; "any organized communities, having a reasonable chance to do anything better, would be politically insane to give up their distinct formations and subject themselves to the domination of Canada."

Realizing the force of the opposition and fearing defeat, both Tupper and Tilley hesitated to place the Quebec Resolutions before their legislatures. But in New Brunswick, Tilley's government had been in power for nearly its full term and soon had to face the voters. He decided to call an election in which Confederation would inevitably be the main issue.

Tilley was on the defensive throughout the campaign. His government was already unpopular with the voters, and its advocacy of Confederation did not increase its support. The anti-Confederates raised the specter of higher taxes and of local businesses unable to compete with cheap goods from central Canada. Roman Catholic leaders were fearful of the aggressive Protestantism of Upper Canada.

About the only advantage Tilley could promise from Confederation was the Intercolonial Railway. But he did not dare say which part of the province it would run through, for fear of opposition from the other parts. There were some who said it

A. J. Smith

40

would never be built, anyway, because the Canadians were notoriously unreliable. The opposition championed another alternative, linking the province's railways with the American network through Maine. This had a powerful appeal to the business community of Saint John, the province's largest city.

When the polls closed on March 6, 1865, it was clear that Confederation had been badly defeated in New Brunswick. Tilley lost his own seat in Saint John, and his party was outnumbered in the new legislature 30–11. The new government of A. J. Smith was solidly against the Quebec Resolutions.

In Nova Scotia, where Confederation was already thought to be "as dead as Julius Caesar," Tupper now more than ever had to avoid the issue. To buy time and distract the opposition he toyed with the idea of reviving Maritime Union as an alternative.

By the spring of 1865 the Confederation scheme had the clear support of only one British North American province, Canada, where it had originated. All four Maritime provinces were either definitely opposed or simply uninterested. The only British North Americans who had been given a chance to vote on the scheme, the New Brunswickers, had turned it down.

All the persuading, bargaining, and speech-making at Charlottetown and Quebec seemed to have been in vain. The new nation seemed to have died before it had a chance to live. "The political destiny of our country," one prominent Canadian wrote, "seems to be involved in utter uncertainty and impenetrable obscurity."

Interventions

The anti-Confederate case in the Maritimes rested on satisfaction with the status quo in British North America. Why rock the boat when it was sailing along so nicely?

If the colonies had been able to isolate themselves from the rest of the world, that kind of provincial contentment might have lasted indefinitely. But in 1865 and 1866 pressures mounted from outside their borders to force a reconsideration of Confederation. The future became uncertain enough that Nova Scotia and New Brunswick had to agree to at least some kind of British North American union.

In the first place, these provinces were still colonies of Great Britain. They were like adolescents in having a wide measure of self-government, but still having to take the wishes of the mother country into account on important questions. They knew they could not win in any ultimate showdown with Great Britain over their destiny unless, like any rebellious adolescent, they were actually prepared to leave home. That would be going too far. For all of their dislike of Confederation, and of British interference in their own affairs, Maritimers were loyal British subjects who would not seriously consider such other possibilities as independence or annexation to the United States.

Britain wanted Confederation. A decade earlier British statesmen had been inclined to consider proposals for a union of their North American colonies as premature. Now in the 1860s they were increasingly worried about the difficulty of defending Canada in any war with the United States. Facing a continually tense situation in Europe, finding relations with the United States perpetually strained during the Civil War (and no better after it ended in 1865), the British government looked favorably on any proposal that might include British North Americans

*Canadian militia called out
to guard the border against
expected Fenian raids, 1866*

taking on more of the responsibility, especially the costs, of defending themselves. Confederation would not be a question of giving up the colonies—although there were loud enough voices in England in the 1860s saying that colonies were useless extravagances. Rather it would be an adminstrative reorganization of the North American provinces, putting them on a more solid financial basis, and relieving the economic burden on Britain for both defense and the costs of government.

British reaction to the Quebec Resolutions was enthusiastic. If the provincial legislatures accepted them, the mother country would quickly pass the necessary legislation. Enthusiasm hardened into impatience when most of the colonials—all those in the Province of Canada—seemed to want a Confederation and only those in the comparatively insignificant Maritime provinces disapproved. "There is something almost ridiculous in the idea of their standing upon an opinion of their own in such a matter against ours, and against that of Canada with five or six times their population," one of the leading British cabinet ministers wrote haughtily. The others agreed. At the urging of the Canadians the British government determined to apply all the pressure it could to change the Maritimers' minds about Confederation.

The lieutenant-governor of Nova Scotia, known to be opposed to Confederation, was replaced by a pro-Confederate with orders to use all his influence in the cause. The lieutenant-governor of New Brunswick, Arthur Hamilton Gordon, was given the same instructions. In June 1865 an imperial dispatch went to each of the provinces declaring "the strong and deliberate opinion" of Her Majesty's Government that Confederation was "an object much to be desired." Pro-Confederate politicians were welcomed and encouraged in London; anti-Confederates coming to plead their case were politely told it was hopeless.

The pressure was most heavily felt in New Brunswick, where A. J. Smith's anti-Confederate government, now in open defiance of British wishes, knew it had to develop a satisfactory alternative to Confederation or soon give in. Many of the anti-Confederates had hoped for closer economic relations with the United States based on railway connections with Maine. But no one could be found to provide the money for the new railway, and the province could not afford to build one itself. More ominously, the Americans had recently acted to dash hopes for increased trade across the border.

In March of 1865 the United States government gave notice that it would not renew the Reciprocity Treaty of 1854 with the British North American provinces. When it expired in 1866, natural products would no longer be traded freely across the border. Partly from a feeling that the treaty had worked to American disadvantage, partly moved by anti-British sentiment, Washington decided to set up substantial tariff barriers against British North American products. Now the Canadians and Maritimers seemed shut out of the huge American market. They would have to cooperate either to increase their trade among themselves or to negotiate a new agreement with the United States—in either case, cooperate. Smith of New Brunswick was shattered by the realization that his province had no hope of renewing reciprocity on its own.

New Brunswick's main alternative to Confederation had disappeared. All Smith could fall back on was continued provincial isolation. Many of his fellow ministers were beginning to realize that some kind of union with Canada was probably inevitable. Smith himself wavered. His government drifted, uncertain and divided.

In the spring of 1866 Lieutenant-Governor Gordon brought the issue to a head. By insisting that the legislature consider Confederation he forced Smith's government into resigning in protest against Gordon's abuse of his power. There would be another election. New Brunswickers would have a second chance to vote on Confederation.

Now another outside force intervened in British North American life. The Fenian Order had been organized in Ireland in 1858 and in the United States in 1859. Its members were devoted to forcibly liberating Ireland from British rule. The Fenians in the United States decided that their best strategy for attacking England would be to invade and conquer British North America. The Fenians began to be taken seriously late in 1865 when the disbanding of the victorious Union armies left thousands of trained Irish-American soldiers footloose and with easy access to weapons.

"Many battles we have won, along with the boys in blue, And we'll go and capture Canada, for we've nothing else to do."

In January and February, 1866, Fenian conventions in the United States rang with wild threats against all things British. By St. Patrick's Day both Canada and Nova Scotia had called out their militia to guard the borders. In April it was New Brunswick's turn to be threatened, as newspapers reported the streets of Portland, Maine, filled with "suspicious looking Americanized Irishmen, carrying revolvers and long dirk knives in their pants' belts." British warships were rushed from Halifax and even from the Mediterranean to patrol the coastal waters. On April 14, five Fenians landed on New Brunswick soil, held up a customs agent at gunpoint, and stole a British flag.

The Fenian threat to New Brunswick and Nova Scotia was greatly exaggerated. One historian has called the leaders "a crew of grandiloquent clowns and vainglorious incompetents," their followers "a crowd of seedy theatrical extras." The only fairly serious Fenian attack took place in June across the Niagara River into Upper Canada, but it was quickly dispersed.

Still, British North Americans had to take the threat seriously. What if the large Irish population in the colonies supported the invaders? What if the American government, always suspected of having annexationist sympathies, actively supported the Fenians, or at least turned a blind eye to their activities? The fact was that Fenianism threatened British North America. It was the most serious threat of invasion and war since 1814.

And it worked wonderfully in the interests of Confederation. This was no time to be even suspected of disloyalty to Britain. It was a time to rally round the flag—"beneath the Union Jack, we'll drive the rabble back"—to swallow petty prejudices and partisan conflict in a show of patriotism. Irish Catholic leaders in the colonies were particularly anxious to disassociate themselves from the irresponsible Fenians. They let it be known that they now approved of Confederation. All Maritimers saw clearly the reality of British power defending their provinces. They understood that it was time to accept British advice about their future.

For over a year Tupper had delayed bringing Confederation before the Nova Scotia legislature while playing for time and working to divide the anti-Confederates. Now he seized the opportunity and rushed a resolution through the assembly authorizing the government to proceed with "a scheme of union which will effectually ensure just provision for the rights and interests of the Province." It was passed at 2:30 A.M. on April 18, "while the Bay of Fundy was alive with ships of war, and the frontier bristling with bayonets." No matter that the anti-Confederates spoke of the betrayal of their province, of a crime carried out in the dead of night. Confederation, or at least some kind of union, had been officially accepted in Nova Scotia.

Tilley and Confederation swept New Brunswick in the election of June, 1866. British pressure, the failure of Smith's railway and trade policy, above all the Fenian menace, had completely discredited the anti-Confederates. On June 30, 1866, the new assembly voted 31–8 in favor of a union "upon such terms as will secure the just rights and interests of New Brunswick." Despite the vagueness of the phrasing, it was well understood that the province had changed its mind on Confederation.

Some of the voters in that 1866 New Brunswick election had had their minds changed by still another group of outsiders. Some $40,000, perhaps more, had been sent down from the Province of Canada to help Tilley win votes. Macdonald and Galt, who had collected "the needful" for Tilley, suspected his opponents were being bankrolled by Americans and anti-Confederate Nova Scotians. In any case they had no qualms about intervening when Confederation hung in the balance. Canada's Fathers of Confederation were practical politicians with few scruples about spending money or using influence for a good cause.

Success

The last act was set in London, the heart of the British Empire. By December 1866 delegations from the three provinces—Canada, New Brunswick, and Nova Scotia—had finally arrived for one last conference to draw up the legislation that the British Parliament would pass to create a new nation.

Whatever Tupper and Tilley had had to say back home about renegotiating the Quebec Resolutions to get better terms, neither Canada nor the British government had any intention of starting the constitution-making all over again. Led by Macdonald as chairman, the delegates built squarely on the foundations of the Quebec Resolutions. The most significant changes were a new guarantee that the educational rights of religious minorities would be protected in the new nation and slightly better financial terms for New Brunswick and Nova Scotia.

The work of the London Conference was technical and uneventful, with time off for visits to English country estates, wining and dining with Britain's greatest statesmen, and Christmas holidaying on the Continent. The most serious "crisis" that occurred during the conference was when John A. Macdonald fell asleep one night with his candle burning and set his bedclothes on fire. Cartier and Galt helped put it out.

At the end of it all there was the question of names. What would the new nation be called? Even the Maritimers agreed that "Canada" was the obvious choice (the two sections of the old Province of Canada would become the new provinces of Ontario and Quebec). Many delegates wanted to use the title "Kingdom of Canada" to show the world that this was a monarchy, governed on quite different principles from the American republic.

*The Centre Block of the Parliament
Buildings under construction, Ottawa, 1866.
Intended to house a provincial legislature,
the buildings became the meeting place
of the Parliament of a new nation.*

The British were afraid that the bold use of "Kingdom" might offend the Americans, who had always been touchy about signs of European influence being exercised in the New World. Rather than open "a monarchical blister on the side of the United States," the delegates were urged to find a less controversial description of their nation. Tilley of New Brunswick is said to have remembered the line from Psalm 72 "He shall have dominion also from sea to sea." So the British kingdom in North America became the "Dominion of Canada." No one thought it was a very exciting title, but at least it was inoffensive to the United States.

The bill to unite British North America passed through the House of Lords and House of Commons without any serious change, or even serious debate. Joseph Howe had rushed to London like a jilted lover trying to stop a marriage on the wedding day. He claimed to speak for 30,000 Nova Scotians who had signed a petition asking to be left out of Confederation. He persuaded a few English politicians to ask why the bill had to be pushed through before the next election in Nova Scotia, when the people would have a chance to express their opinion. These objections were ignored.

Many people in Britain ignored the whole debate. A troublesome colonial situation was being fixed. Now Britain wouldn't have to bother itself with North America. Only Lord Carnarvon, the colonial secretary who guided the legislation through the House of Lords, caught a vision of the future. "We are laying the foundations of a great state," he said, "perhaps one which at a future day may even overshadow this country. But, come what may, we shall rejoice that we have shown neither indifference to their wishes, nor jealousy of their aspirations, but that we honestly and sincerely, to the utmost of our power and knowledge, fostered their growth, recognizing in it the conditions of our greatness."

Queen Victoria signed the British North America Act on March 29, 1867. This was the constitution of the Dominion of Canada. It came into effect on July 1, 1867.

From Sea to Sea

George Brown had left the coalition, satisfied that "Rep by Pop" had come at last. Sir John A. Macdonald was Canada's first prime minister. Cartier, sulking a bit because he had not been knighted, stayed on as Macdonald's French-Canadian lieutenant. Tupper and Tilley were the government's most prominent Maritime supporters. For them the end was only the beginning. On July 1, 1867, the Dominion had only four provinces and did not extend from sea to sea.

Macdonald's new government set out to finish the job. One aim was to add all the rest of the British territories in North America to Canada. Another aim was to put flesh on the bones of the skeleton nation, to make it possible for Ontarians, Quebecers, and Maritimers to come to think of themselves as Canadians first.

In 1869 Canada completed an arrangement to take over all the territories formerly governed by the Hudson's Bay Company. It would now have its great western hinterland, stretching to the Rockies, the new frontier. The Province of Manitoba was created in the west in 1870 as a result of a brief uprising by the Métis (half-breed) inhabitants whose rights had been ignored in the transfer. In 1905, after a great influx of settlers, the rolling prairies west of Manitoba became the provinces of Saskatchewan and Alberta.

On the Pacific coast the two British colonies of Vancouver Island and British Columbia had enjoyed a brief period of prosperity with the discovery of gold in the late 1850s. As the gold rush died, though, the region stagnated and the colonial governments became desperate for economic assistance. Vancouver Island became part of British Columbia in 1866, and in

Driving the last spike in the Canadian
Pacific Railway, November 7, 1885.
The Dominion is at last tied together.

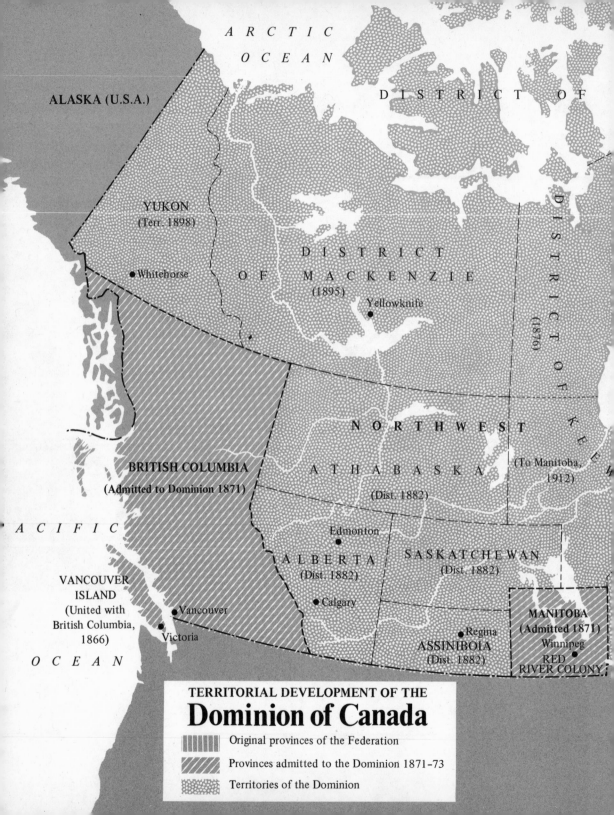

ARCTIC
OCEAN

ALASKA (U.S.A.)

DISTRICT OF

YUKON
(Terr. 1898)

•Whitehorse

DISTRICT
OF MACKENZIE
(1895)

Yellowknife•

DISTRICT OF KEE

(1876)

BRITISH COLUMBIA

(Admitted to Dominion 1871)

NORTHWEST

ATHABASKA
(Dist. 1882)

(To Manitoba,
1912)

PACIFIC

Edmonton•

ALBERTA
(Dist. 1882)

SASKATCHEWAN
(Dist. 1882)

VANCOUVER
ISLAND
(United with
British Columbia,
1866)

•Calgary

•Vancouver
•Victoria

•Regina

ASSINIBOIA
(Dist. 1882)

MANITOBA
(Admitted 1871)
Winnipeg
•
RED
RIVER COLONY

OCEAN

TERRITORIAL DEVELOPMENT OF THE
Dominion of Canada

Original provinces of the Federation

Provinces admitted to the Dominion 1871–73

Territories of the Dominion

FRANKLIN
(1895)

GREENLAND
(Denmark)

ATLANTIC

OCEAN

HUDSON

BAY

TERRITORIES
(Ceded to Canada by
Hudson's Bay Company, 1870)

DISTRICT
OF
UNGAVA

LABRADOR
To Newfoundland

(To Newfoundland,
1927)

(To Quebec, 1912)

St. John's
NEWFOUNDLAND
(Admitted to Dominion
1949)

TIN

(To Ontario, 1912)

QUEBEC
(1867)

PRINCE
EDWARD
ISLAND
1873
Charlottetown

NEW
BRUNSWICK
1867

NOVA SCOTIA
(1867)

Quebec

Frederickton

Halifax

Montreal

Ottawa

ONTARIO
(1867)

Toronto

UNITED   STATES

1871 the whole of British Columbia joined Canada. Now the Dominion was finally a nation from the Atlantic to the Pacific, *"ab mare usque ad mare."* These Westerners had few natural ties with the Canadians, but looked to Confederation as a means of ensuring a prosperous future. The greatest Canadian project of the 1870s and 1880s was to build a transcontinental railway, the Canadian Pacific, to tie the nation together with links of steel.

Railways also caused Prince Edward Island's entry into the Dominion. When the Island built its own railway and found it could not afford the costs involved, it negotiated terms of union. In 1873 the Islanders who had rejected the scheme born in their own capital swallowed their proud independence and became Canadians.

All Maritimers finally had rail connection with central Canada when the Intercolonial, begun immediately after Confederation, was opened in 1876.

Absentmindedly Canada took over Britain's claims to the Arctic Islands north of its territory in 1880. It took almost a century for Canadians to realize that the far north was their last and (because of its gas, oil, and minerals) perhaps richest frontier.

The fishermen of Newfoundland fought the Atlantic and ignored the mainland for more than eighty years after Confederation. Finally realizing that there was no future except poverty and emigration unless the Island could share in the wealth and social welfare policies of Canada, the Newfoundlanders joined the Dominion in 1949. More than one hundred years after 1867 Canada still had a living Father of Confederation in Joey Smallwood, leader of the union movement in Newfoundland and the province's first premier.

One of the most eloquent Fathers of Confederation had not lived to see any of these developments. On April 7, 1868, D'Arcy McGee was shot and killed outside his Ottawa house. He was one of only two Canadian politicians ever to be assassinated. His last speech in the House of Commons had been a plea for patience in working out Canada's problems.

ARCTIC
OCEAN

ALASKA (U.S.A.)

DISTRICT OF

YUKON
(Terr. 1898)

⊛ Whitehorse

NORTHWEST

DISTRICT OF
MACKENZIE

DIST-
OF
KEEWATIN

⊛ Yellowknife

PACIFIC

BRITISH
COLUMBIA
(1871)

ALBERTA
(1905)

MANITOBA
(1871)

Edmonton
⊛

SASKATCHEWAN
(1905)

● Calgary

Victoria ● Vancouver
⊛

OCEAN

Regina ⊛

Winnipeg ⊛

Canada Today

⊛ Provincial capitals and administrative centers

(Dates after names of provinces show admission
to the Federation)

GREENLAND

F R A N K L I N

T E R R I T O R I E S

R I C T

H U D S O N

B A Y

A T L A N T I C

O C E A N

NEWFOUNDLAND

LABRADOR

St.John's ✳

(Admitted to
Dominion, 1949)

Q U E B E C
(1867)

**PRINCE
EDWARD
ISLAND
1873**

O N T A R I O
(1867)

✳ Charlottetown

**NEW
BRUNSWICK
1867**

**NOVA SCOTIA
1867**

Quebec ✳

Frederickton ✳

✳ Halifax

Montreal ●

✳ Ottawa

Toronto
✳

U N I T E D   S T A T E S

Afterward

Neither at Confederation nor afterward did Canadians develop a strong sense of identity. As the Confederation movement itself showed, it was a nation built in diversity. There were two founding races and languages, English and French; two quite different regions, the Province of Canada and the Maritimes (and later a third, the Northwest); two levels of government, federal and provincial. There was a massive amount of territory, half a continent.

The land could be tamed by steel rails, settlers' ploughs, and the daring of the bush pilot. The sense of racial and regional identity could not so easily be overcome. Except in wartime the people chose to think of themselves as English or French, Maritimers, Quebecers, or Westerners, as often as they realized they were Canadians. Nova Scotians (whose first response to Confederation in 1867 was to ask to get out of it) still muttered about secession as late as the 1920s. French-Canadians never forgot the Conquest; Quebec separatism became a powerful movement in the 1960s. The Métis uprising of 1869–1870 was only the first expression of a sense of Western dissatisfaction that has continued to the present. Canadians have often wondered if their nation had any natural reason for existing at all, whether it was a logical political unit based on the St. Lawrence–Great Lakes waterway, or merely an artificial bundle of separate regions and races.

It had been difficult to achieve a union of the British North American provinces in the first place. The constitution had been deliberately vague about the future of the provinces and the debates had been confused. Maritime reluctance had been beaten down by pressure and subterfuge and the Fenian scare—though Canada was one of the few nineteenth-century nations not born in violence. (Is that why both students and teachers have so often complained about its history being dull?) Thoughtful observers of the Confederation movement of the 1860s would not have been surprised at the resurgence of regionalism after 1867, particularly the tendency of the provincial governments to increase in power as the guardians of racial and regional interests against the centralizing tendencies of Ottawa.

Governing Canada became a perpetual balancing act. John A. Macdonald, who died in office in 1891, was remembered as the best balancer of all, the sometimes tipsy father of the country. The chief responsibility of his successors, including three French-Canadians, was to maintain unity among the regions, races, and religious groups.

The sphere of Canadian self-government gradually expanded until complete formal independence from Great Britain was recognized by the Statute of Westminster of 1931. In the twentieth century Canada played a full role in the world community in its own right, although as a member of the British Commonwealth linked symbolically to Britain by the monarchy.

Often united only by their diversity and their determination to remain separate from the United States, Canadians are among the world's most fortunate people in terms of material wealth because of the richness of their land's natural resources. At almost all times after 1867 they have enjoyed the most important legacy of the Fathers of Confederation—a political system that gave them, in the words of the British North America Act, "Peace, Order and good Government."

Bibliography

Browne, G. P., ed. *Documents on the Confederation of British North America*. Toronto: McClelland and Stewart, 1969.

Careless, J. M. S. *Brown of The Globe,* 2 vols. Toronto: Macmillan, 1959, 1963.

Creighton, Donald. *The Road to Confederation*. Toronto: Macmillan, 1964.

————. *John A. Macdonald: The Young Politician*. Toronto: Macmillan, 1952.

Morton, W. L. *The Critical Years: The Union of British North America, 1857–1873*. Toronto: McClelland and Stewart, 1964.

Waite, P. B. *The Charlottetown Conference, 1864*. Ottawa: Canadian Historical Association Booklets, No. 15, 1963.

————. *The Life and Times of Confederation, 1864–1867*. Toronto: University of Toronto Press, 1962.

Whitelaw, W. M. *The Quebec Conference*. Ottawa: Canadian Historical Association Booklets, No. 20, 1966.

Index